Called to Serve

✠ ✠ ✠

A Spirituality for Deacons

Phyllis Zagano, Ph.D.

D1392430

Liguori
ONE LIGUORI DRIVE
LIGUORI MO 63057-9999

Imprimi Potest:
Richard Thibodeau, C.Ss.R.
Provincial, Denver Province
The Redemptorists

ISBN 0-7648-1133-9
© 2004, Liguori Publications
Printed in the United States of America
04 05 06 07 08 5 4 3 2 1

Imprimatur:
Most Reverend Robert J. Hermann
Auxiliary Bishop
Archdiocese of St. Louis

Excerpts from the *New American Bible* with Revised New Testament and Psalms Copyright © 1986, 1970 Confraternity of Christian Doctrine, Inc., Washington, DC. Used with permission. All rights reserved. No portion of the *New American Bible* may be reprinted without permission in writing from the copyright holder.

Excerpts from the English translation of the *Rites of Ordination of a Bishop, of Priests, and of Deacons (Second Typical Edition)* © 2000, 2002, International Committee on English in the Liturgy, Inc. All rights reserved.

Lyrics from "Ubi Caritas" copyright © by Les Presses de Taizé (France). Used by permission of GIA Publications, exclusive agent. All rights reserved.

All rights reserved. No part of this booklet may be reproduced, stored in a retrieval system, or transmitted without the written permission of Liguori Publications.

To order, call 1-800-325-9521
www.liguori.org

Contents

✠ ✠ ✠

About the Author

Dr. Phyllis Zagano is author or editor of ten books, including *On Prayer: A Letter to My Godchild* (Liguori 2001), published in Spanish as *Acerca de la oración: Una carta a mi ahijada* (Liguori, 2003). Her book, *Holy Saturday: An Argument for the Restoration of the Female Diaconate in the Catholic Church* (Crossroad 2000), received a First Place Book Award from the Catholic Press Association (2001) and the College Theology Society Book Award (2002). Her books have been variously translated into Czech, Indonesian, Italian, and Spanish. Dr. Zagano is a popular speaker at theological meetings and conferences. She teaches religious studies at Hofstra University, Hempstead, New York.

The Diaconate Matters

✠ ✠ ✠

The Lord has a wonderful way of reminding me what is important. Many times, in the middle of a radio interview or after I have delivered a detailed presentation about the ordination of women to the diaconate, the question comes up: "What does it matter whether someone is ordained a deacon or not? After all, anyone can do what a deacon does."

Here I am presenting history, ecclesiology, canon law, and sacramental theology, hoping that people will understand the diaconate, maybe even expand it a little bit, and what I hear is, "It doesn't matter."

But it does matter. Deacons make a real difference in the Church today, and ordination is a great part of the reason for the difference. If you are a deacon reading this, I mean that you, deeply and personally the unique you, make a real difference in the Church. If you are a deacon candidate or someone thinking about the diaconate, you too are making a difference because you are thinking and praying about a ministry as old as the Church itself. Whether you eventually join the ministry of the Church in this particular way or not, your interest can be lifelong support for others who have been so called. And you and they do make a real difference.

What kind of difference? There are many functions in the Church that may only be provided by deacons, as well as by priests or bishops. That is, there are many functions in the Church that are reserved to clerics. We focus so often on the need for priests and priestly ministry, and the role and functions of bishops and episcopal leadership, that we forget that the Word, the liturgy, and charity are specifically served by deacons. And only deacons are deacons.

But deacons cannot fill the real needs of the Church, the argument goes. Well, too often we tend to focus on what deacons cannot do, even with regard to clerical authority. A deacon may not be the pastor of a parish. A deacon may not celebrate Eucharist, hear sacramental confessions, or anoint the sick.

The positive response is stunningly simple: deacons are not meant to substitute for priests. Deacons are ordained to ministry, not to priesthood. When we focus specifically on what a deacon can do, we find there are many administrative and sacramental tasks deacons may share with other clergy. For example, a deacon may be a single judge in a tribunal. A deacon is an ordinary minister of the Eucharist. A deacon can witness marriages and solemnly baptize. A deacon may preach at any liturgy.

"But, but," the questioner sputters on, "there is nothing about these things that an ordinary lay person cannot do. There are many lay canon lawyers. Lay people serve as Eucharistic ministers. Lay people in mission territories often have permission to marry and to baptize. There are lay pastoral administrators. And lay people preach at liturgies, whether the bishop likes it or not."

Well, all this is true. But there is still the particular charism of orders and the sacramental reality of ordination. As a Church, we believe in the mystery of grace in individual lives. We believe that through the charism of orders the deacon lives supported by this particular grace. The deacon has made a public and permanent commitment to the Church, to the people of God. The charism of orders both identifies and strengthens the ordained deacon as a servant of the body of Christ. The deacon, sacramentally ordained to serve the people of God, is steward of the Word. The deacon is a minister of the liturgy. The deacon has a special mandate to help the poor and all in need in charity.

Unfortunately, many people in this wonderful Church of ours simply cannot figure the diaconate out. They may imagine that deacons are merely super altar boys or failed priests. They may wonder if the diaconate is just the next step up after parish council or the last step before priesthood.

These questions float in and out of parish halls, through academic centers, even around episcopal offices. There is widespread misunderstanding about the diaconate in the United States in every quarter of Church life. There need not be. The fact of the matter is, there is one sacred order of deacons, which is exercised for a short period of time by transitional deacons. Most deacons live the diaconate as a permanent rank of the hierarchy in both the Latin and the Eastern Catholic Churches.

And there are many deacons. Since the re-establishment of the permanent diaconate by Pope Paul VI *(Ad Pascendum,* 1972), over 26,000 married and celibate men, secular and religious, have been ordained to the diaconate as their separate and permanent vocation. Most serve in developed nations, over half serve in the United States and Canada. They live a full and equal order distinct from priesthood: "At a lower level of the hierarchy are to be found deacons, who receive the imposition of hands 'not for the priesthood, but for the ministry'" *(Lumen Gentium,* 29). The specific tasks of the priest or bishop in which he acts *in persona Christi* belong to the priest or bishop alone. The deacon joins the priest and bishop in the services rendered to and on behalf of the community, rendered *in nomine ecclesiae,* in the name of the Church. Through it all, the deacon lives the special charism of service through the ministry and not through priestly acts. The deacon is called to serve.

In fact, the very word *diakonia,* from which we have received the word *deacon,* means service. We find this word in Mark's Gospel, presenting the vocation of Jesus: "For the Son of Man did not come to be served but to serve and to give his life as a ransom for many" (Mark 10:45). These most serious words reflect on the call of every Christian and in particular on the call of the deacon. The *diakonia* required here implies the self-emptying exemplified by Christ's sacrifice and implies it without reference to priestly acts.

As a permanent rank of the hierarchy in our churches, the diaconate has been a vital force for the service of the people of God. Ordained to the Word, the liturgy, and charity, the deacon puts on Christ in a special way, as servant called to justice.

Questions For Reflection

1. How has the diaconate made a difference in your life?
2. How has the diaconate made a difference in the life of the Church?
3. How does Jesus present the model for the diaconate?

Diaconal Spirituality

✠ ✠ ✠

As minister of the Word, the liturgy, and charity, the deacon becomes the conscience of the people and of the hierarchy, constantly calling each to social justice and charity. But how does one get from here to there? What comprises a spirituality of the diaconate?

The essential Christian vocation is signified by baptism. We are called to new life in Christ through baptism and by living our baptismal promises. As baptized Christians we live and breathe the Word of God, celebrate its witness in the liturgy, and joyfully live the lives of Christian charity we have been led to through the Gospel. Our lives follow the pattern of creation-redemption-sanctification. We recognize ourselves as creatures, beloved of God. We know ourselves as redeemed by Christ. We strive to live as a resurrected people, sanctified through the grace of the Spirit.

The deacon lives this essential Christian vocation with a particular intensity. Called to a life
of prayer and service, the deacon recognizes
the continual pattern of created-redeemed-
sanctified in his own life and in the lives of
others. He hears his own call many places,
perhaps especially in the well-known story of
the call of Samuel (1 Samuel 3:1-20). The story
of Samuel's vocation can pierce the heart of
anyone time and time again. Samuel is serv-
ing Yahewh "in the presence of Eli," who is
older and more experienced in the ways of the
Lord. Samuel hears a call at night, and assumes
it is his master. It is not. Three times Samuel
rises in the night and goes to Eli, who kindly
explains to Samuel that the call is not from
Eli, but from God. And so Eli tells Samuel,
"Go to sleep, and if you are called, reply,
'Speak, LORD, for your servant is listening'"
(3:9). And that is what Samuel does. Surpris-
ingly, God's words to Samuel are not that com-
forting. For God tells Samuel that his beloved
master Eli, and his entire family, will be
condemned for cursing God. Nothing can
expiate their guilt.

Samuel's assignment is difficult. He loves
Eli, but the Lord directs him to give his

master the bad news. So Samuel passes along Yahweh's promise of condemnation, and Eli responds: "He is the LORD. He will do what he judges best" (3:18).

How precious the gift of Eli's wisdom! Samuel is still young and still learning his vocation. He has given his master, Eli, the worst possible news: he and his entire family will be condemned. Yet Eli remains in awe of God, and cannot doubt the sentence: "He is the LORD. He will do what he judges best." What a stunning second lesson for young Samuel!

So Samuel grew, and kept the word of God with him. We know from Scripture that Samuel listened carefully to the Lord and that "the LORD was with him, not permitting any word of his to be without effect" (3:19). How beautiful an image! Samuel carried the word of God like precious stones or fragile flowers. Not a single one fell to the ground. Once Samuel learned how to listen to the word of God at the feet of his master, he held it close to his heart and brought its message to the people of God. Hence Samuel was known throughout the land as a prophet of the Lord.

This is what the deacon does. Not every

deacon is a prophet, of course, but every deacon is part prophet. Every deacon learns to recognize the voice of the Lord in his own heart and carries the word of God to the people. Learning how to do this is not easy, but not hard either. That is what "formation" means—conforming the mind and heart to God and learning how to act on it. From that base diaconal spirituality grows. To conform the mind and heart to God, the deacon presents himself, his whole being, prayerfully before the Lord daily in the consideration of Scripture. Such profound presentation is not "useful," not utilitarian, but rather the sort of "useless" time wasted walking along the seashore with an old friend. The precious minutes and hours the deacon spends in prayerful reflection on the Word of God will connect to his preaching and teaching, but in an indirect and powerfully intimate way. More importantly, it will help form him as a deacon.

Questions for Reflection

1. What parallels, if any, do you see between the call of Samuel and your own vocation?
2. What role does Scripture play in your unique relationship with God?
3. Do you regularly pray with Scripture?

Formation and the Spiritual Life

✠ ✠ ✠

P rayer is at the root of all formation, and prayer is sometimes hard to describe. Saint John Vianney, the famous nineteenth-century French confessor, describes prayer this way:

> Prayer is nothing else but union with God. When one has a heart that is pure and united with God, he is given a kind of serenity and sweetness that makes him ecstatic, a light that surrounds him with marvelous brightness. In this intimate union, God and the soul are fused together like two bits of wax that no one can ever pull apart. This union of God with a tiny creature is a lovely thing. It is a happiness beyond understanding.[1]

The goal of formation is to create the situation in which "God and the soul are fused together like two bits of wax that no one can ever pull apart." Formation is a serious undertaking, and it is exactly what it sounds like— the change of mind and heart, the conformation of one's entire being to the mind of God. Formation also involves the subtle (and sometimes non-so-subtle) changes in personality that allow the minister to perform ministry and not get in the way of God's desires, for both himself and others. That is, formation brings us to the place where we are quite comfortable decreasing and only too happy to see Christ increasing, in our own lives, in the individual lives of people, and in the world at large.

Formal formation to the diaconate involves formation in the four competencies common both to priestly and to lay ministry formation— human, spiritual, intellectual, and pastoral. Human growth and development, intellectual work in theological sciences, and pastoral training each bring the deacon to a new level of awareness of his vocation and increase his ability to serve God's people. Spiritual formation and diaconal spirituality—a life in the Spirit—bind the other three areas together.

Spiritual Directors and Confessors

No one undergoes formation alone. Most especially, no one undergoes spiritual formation alone. At the outset, the optimal situation is for the deacon-candidate to come to the decision to enter the diaconal training program after prayerful reflection with a trained spiritual director, to continue spiritual direction throughout his training program, and to maintain a practice of regular spiritual direction throughout the rest of his life.

Choosing a spiritual director is not the same as choosing a confessor. While some individuals have the same person as both confessor and director, others find it better to separate the two ministries. Choosing a director, like choosing a regular confessor, is serious business. The confessor, like the director, can play no role in determining the deacon candidate's readiness for ordination, because each is involved in the "internal forum" and only matter from the "external forum" can be considered. Neither would one's spiritual director or confessor ordinarily be a supervisor or a colleague. When you think about it, this makes sense, because to approach the sacrament of reconciliation and to approach spiritual direction, one must be free. While both the director and the confessor respond in conversation within the boundaries of their respective ministries, neither may act on the information he or she discusses with the directee. That is, the matter of both spiritual direction and of confession is sacrosanct. The difference is that in a following session of spiritual direction, the director may bring up prior conversations with the directee. Generally speaking, the confessor may not.

Confessors are often nominated by formation programs, but confessors are always freely chosen by penitents. Different persons have different preferences. Some go to monasteries, where confession is heard daily and often. Some have found a good confessor in the next parish.

Spiritual directors, likewise, are sometimes nominated by formation programs and often chosen in other ways. There are many persons out there who consider themselves spiritual directors, but some have had less training than others, or even no training at all. The best way to choose a spiritual director (not to be confused with a confessor) is to ask about for recommendations, and then go to see for yourself. The initial interview with a spiritual director is really a two-way interview to see if this other Christian is the person who can accompany you prayerfully in your spiritual life. You have the right to ask pertinent questions of your potential director, and the first two should be "Are you in regular spiritual direction?" and "Are you under supervision?"

Most people who are serious about their spiritual lives see a spiritual director about every four weeks or so, generally stretched no more than six weeks from time to time when holidays, vacations, bad weather, or simple scheduling difficulties intervene. That means that the director must be in such a regular relationship, precisely as the directee seeks to enter one. Supervision of spiritual directors is quite serious business and comprises regular one-hour meetings with a qualified supervisor of spiritual directors, the purpose of which is to clarify any spiritual issues arising from the director's work and to free the director to prayerfully listen to the spiritual life of another.

Retreats and Days of Prayer

Retreats and days of prayer are an integral part of formative spirituality and of ongoing formation. The annual retreat recommended for all clerics can take many forms. Some dioceses sponsor retreats for deacons and their wives. While practice varies, there is much to be said for a silent directed retreat, whereby the retreatant spends his days in silent reflection on God's Word in Scripture, as directed by the director. In the daily interview with the director, the retreatant discusses the content of the prior day's prayer. Directed retreats can be six, or seven, or eight days long. Eight-day retreats are most often those that follow the pattern of the Spiritual Exercises of St. Ignatius of Loyola (1491-1556), founder of the Society of Jesus (Jesuits).

Ignatius was an eminently practical person, and he learned the common elements of the human spiritual journey through his own extended pilgrimage. His Spiritual Exercises, commonly understood as the thirty-day retreat, or "the long retreat" really comprise a handbook about the interior movements of the soul for the director. In a thirty-day or even in an eight-day Ignatian retreat, the individual is guided at his own pace through the major steps (referred to as "weeks") in the repeated pattern of our lives—creation, redemption, sanctification, with special emphasis where needed in one or another week. The graces attendant to each week—whether in recognition of the glory of our own creation, or in gratitude for the salvific action of Christ in our lives and in consideration of how that can be repaid, or in sorrow for the corruptions of the world and of ourselves, or in recognition and gratitude for our own redemption through Christ—are always specific to our own needs and our own situations. Hence the carefully directed retreat is important to personal spiritual growth. Where possible, many people choose to be directed in retreat by the same individual who assists them with their ongoing spiritual formation as their regular director. This is not always possible, and so retreat houses often ask for a simple paragraph about one's spiritual journey before assigning a director who will pray for and with you in retreat.

The Examen

One daily practice crucial to development of a life in Christ is the daily examen, or examination of consciousness. There are various ways to enter into this short prayerful review of the day. Mother Teresa taught the easiest way. At the end of the day, she said, count out these five words of Christ on the fingers of one hand: "You did this to me." To recall every action, every thought, in that light is at first a startling revelation, but at once it is the essence of a very developed spirituality. Other methods abound. Some suggest a pause in the midst of night prayer, for ten minutes or so, equally to review the day, inside and out. It is important not to get too negative in this practice; too careful housecleaning can lead to pride. The Ignatian examen takes about fifteen minutes, and comprises five simple steps:

1. Recall you are in the presence of God.
2. Look at your day with gratitude.
3. Ask help from the Holy Spirit.
4. Review your day.
5. Reconcile and resolve.

This way of looking at the interior movements of the soul is not so much a review of where things went wrong but rather an exercise in learning the interior movements of the heart. Yes, things pop up every evening that we wish we never did or said, but the Ignatian examen essentially begins with a great big "thank you" for the day. Gratitude is a tremendous thing to learn, and it is a wonderful antidote to pride.

Spiritual Growth

The inevitable result of seriously living a genuine spiritual life is often startling. When an individual fully enters into the life of Christ through prayer, as carefully examined periodically along with a director, the world comes into sharp focus. Things that matter suddenly stand out, away from things that do not matter. People become more important, especially more important than oneself. The gospel becomes the fuel for every conversation, every decision, every movement, and every act. I do not mean that people become pious, but rather they become real. At first the measure of our acts against the Gospel causes great dismay, even a sort of depression. As the Velveteen Rabbit knew, "One runs the risk of crying a little if one lets oneself become real." But as soon as you accept the human condition in yourself, you find you are a little kinder to the next person.

With a developed spirituality, people become real, really real, and live as transparent witnesses to the resurrection in their own and other's lives. Quite frankly, they are not what in common parlance are called "phonies." They live right from wrong; they treat others with respect. Most important, they measure all their acts against the Lord and not against whatever small or large gain they may or may not obtain for themselves or for whatever society they may belong to. So, suddenly they cannot lie. They cannot backbite. They cannot give the little twists in conversation that make the other feel so sad. They do not have to. They have attained a healthy spirituality that plants them firmly and securely in who they are before the Lord.

Such internal guidance and genuine security in God and God's plan is most important to the deacon, because the essence of diaconal spirituality is to be within "the system" yet not of it. That is, the deacon very specifically ministers to and in the name of the people of God, whom he represents through his specific configuration to Christ by baptism and ordination. But the deacon can never forget his identification with the people. Every ministry he performs, whether as minister of the Word, minister of the liturgy, or minister of charity, is done by and for the people of God with whom he is so closely identified.

The deacon, become and constantly becoming real, will face the realities of Church and of the world both guided and protected by the Gospel. His words, like those of Jeremiah, may be upsetting. But it is God who "touched his mouth," saying, 'See, I place my words in your mouth'" (Jeremiah 1:9). The overpowering reality of God's word both is reality and makes sense of it. For what spirituality is all about is holiness, and, at its root, holiness is simply dealing with reality. All Christians, and clerics especially, are obliged to seek holiness in their lives, in their prayer, in the way they relate to others, and in the way they relate to themselves. It is not that easy. But neither is it all that hard.

Questions for Reflection

1. Do your spiritual practices support your vocation?
2. How does prayer become action in your life?
3. Would spiritual direction help you in your life of prayer?

Minister of the Word

✠ ✠ ✠

At ordination, the deacon receives the Book of the Gospels from his bishop, who says, "Receive the Gospel of Christ, whose herald you have become. Believe what you read, teach what you believe, and practice what you teach."[2]

Church documents formalize the deacon's task and relate it to the Word. Specifically, *Lumen Gentium* presents three *munera*—tasks connected to orders and specifically understood in the office of the deacon: *munus docendi* (teaching); *munus sanctificandi* (sanctifying), and *munus regendi* (leading). Through the first, the *munus docendi*, the deacon is marked as a preacher and teacher: "In reference to the *munus docendi*, the deacon is called to proclaim the Scriptures and instruct and exhort the people."[3]

Prayer and Service

But what makes him able to preach? And what makes him able to teach? The conundrum of diaconal spirituality is also its strength: how can one separate the ministry of the Word, from the ministry of the liturgy, from the ministry of charity? Each part of the threefold ministry depends upon the other. So, the deacon can preach and teach because he knows Christ in Scripture deeply and intimately through prayer, reflection, and study. The deacon can preside in sanctifying actions of the Church, representing the whole Church, because of his intimate identification with Christ. And the deacon can animate the life of charity of his parish or his diocese or his religious order's mission through that same identification with the Christ he knows so well through Scripture and whom he represents in the Church when he participates in or leads liturgies.

Above all, the Word of God both calls and allows the deacon to live a life of justice and of charity for and on behalf of the whole Church, the people of God. He comes to that life through prayer, and because he lives such a life, he is able to represent the people of God in liturgy.

This point cannot be overemphasized: the deacon comes to the life of justice and charity through prayer and only through prayer, and he has a special relationship with the Word of God in Scripture. Because the deacon is charged to pray the Liturgy of the Hours, to study and meditate on Scripture, and to preach and teach the Word of God, his entire being is subsumed in the story of the Gospel. Through grace he knows that his own life and the lives of all he meets reflect and repeat the divine cycle of creation, redemption, and sanctification. He sees in his own life the beauty of his own creation; he knows in his own history the grace of Christ's redeeming action in his life; he sees the suffering Jesus in himself and in all whom he meets; and he knows the combined promise of the Incarnation and the Resurrection in his own life.

He lives, above all, as a person of prayer. Through prayer, and especially through meditation on Scripture, the deacon is able to joyfully embody a particular apostolic spirituality appropriate to his ministry. He is sent forth by his bishop or religious superior to breathe the Word of God into every corner of his mission, to formally celebrate its breaking into people's lives, to call forth and to participate in the common Christian call to justice and charity. There is not really any specific job description for the deacon on this apostolic journey. The deacon does whatever is necessary, whatever is needed.[4] He does so with joy.

Prayer and the Apostolic Life

How does this come about? If the deacon ministers to the needs of God's people out of human kindness, he is no different from a social worker. But if his ministry is centered in the Gospel, and rooted in the work of the Church, his endeavors are then apostolic. Hence, the deacon must live and preach the Word of God implanted in his heart that has been nurtured by prayer. Diaconal ministry then becomes the embodiment of the Gospel, the function of the Word made flesh in the person of the deacon, and the result of the self-emptying lived in imitation of Christ.

This happens when the deacon breathes in the Word of God and makes it his very own. It is in the recitation of the main hours of the day—Morning Prayer, Midday Prayer, Evening Prayer, Night Prayer and the Office of Readings—that the deacon both nourishes his own life with God and prays in union with the whole Church on behalf of the people of God, for whom such prayer is often impossible. The deacon, in his attentiveness to the Word, both prays for and represents the people.

The ordaining bishop's charge to each deacon is the heart of his ministry: "Receive the Gospel of Christ, whose herald you have become. Believe what you read, teach what you believe, and practice what you teach." Charged to a new and special relationship with the Gospel, the deacon recognizes the need to bring the Gospel to every area of his life. He tests his own thoughts in the light of the Word. Similarly, he tests his own actions. Bound by mission and ministry in communion with the Holy Father and his own bishop, the deacon both shines light on the Word of God and is in fact that shining light, ordained "to proclaim the Gospel and preach the word of God."[5]

Questions for Reflection

1. How did you understand yourself today as created and beloved of God?
2. How did you understand yourself today as redeemed and beloved of God?
3. How did you understand yourself today as made holy and beloved of God?

Minister of Liturgy

✠ ✠ ✠

The role of the deacon in the community is symbolized in the liturgy. While he is called to speak on behalf of those most in need of justice, he does so because his ministry outside the liturgy in some way enables the powerless, deprived, and marginalized to work effectively for their own development and liberation. His daily work—whether it is full time or part time in the Church's social service agencies, or as teacher, catechist, pastoral worker, or chaplain—allows his to be the voice of the voiceless. He serves the people of God in whatever way he can, in obedience to his bishop and in consideration of his talents and responsibilities. Discerning his specific diaconal ministry in the light of those talents and responsibilities, he knows Paul's advice:

There are different kinds of spiritual gifts but the same Spirit; there are different forms of service but the same Lord; there are different workings but the same God who produces all of them in everyone. (1 Corinthians 12:4-6)

The deacon's life embodies the gospel promise; the gospel promise allows him to speak for those who cannot. The deacon is, in large measure, the bishop's most active representative to the poor, the marginalized, and all who are in need. He represents the social conscience of the Church in its daily ministry to those whom society rejects. As such, whether he is a celibate secular or religious, or married, he lives simply as countercultural witness to worldwide consumerism. Simplicity of life allows him to "stand beside the underprivileged, to practice solidarity with their efforts to create a more just society, to be more sensitive and capable of understanding and discerning realities involving the economic and social aspect of life, and to promote a preferential option for the poor."[6] Simplicity frees him for these gospel tasks.

As servant of the members of the body of

Christ, the deacon represents them and speaks on their behalf in the Mass.

> In the Eucharistic Sacrifice, the deacon does not celebrate the mystery: rather he effectively represents on the one hand, the people of God and, specifically, helps them to unite their lives to the offering of Christ; while on the other, in the name of Christ himself, he helps the Church to participate in the fruits of that sacrifice.[7]

In the Liturgy of the Word, the deacon addresses the people and speaks on their behalf. In the ancient Church, it was the deacon who removed the people's gifts of bread and wine from the church storehouses and who processed with the gifts to the altar.

Throughout the Mass, the deacon's role in society as the minister of and to the people is symbolized. The deacon proclaims the Gospel, and, if authorized by the bishop, the deacon preaches. The deacon presents the prayers of the faithful. The deacon prepares the gifts for the sacrifice. The deacon calls for the kiss of peace. The deacon raises the cup at the elevation, the great symbolic offering of the gifts on behalf of all the people at the conclusion of the anaphora. The deacon is the pre-eminent minister of the cup at the distribution of Eucharist. The deacon dismisses the people.

There are a number of liturgies that may be led by deacons—baptisms, marriage ceremonies, wake services, committal ceremonies, Liturgy of the Hours, and benediction among them. In each the deacon serves on behalf of the pastor, who in turn represents the bishop in his parish.

Questions for Reflection

1. **Who are the voiceless who need your voice?**
2. **How are the needs of people reflected and addressed in the liturgy?**
3. **What can you do to encourage participation in liturgies?**

Minister of Charity

✠ ✠ ✠

Before he does anything else, because he prays and before he preaches, the deacon lives a life of charity.

You may have heard the Taizé chant "Ubi Caritas." Once you have heard it and sung it, you will never forget it. "*Ubi caritas, et amor; ubi caritas, Deus ibi est.*" "Wherever there is charity, and love, there is God." Just as the rhythm, the music, and the words sink into our very beings, so also does the notion that God is truly made present through a ministry of charity and of love. God is not restricted here, to the altar, the ambo, or the pulpit. God is anywhere—wherever—charity and love abide.

It seems to me that this is such an important notion, especially regarding the diaconate, that we must at the outset understand that the deacon's ministry of charity flows from his love of the Word. It is the Word on which the deacon acts. The deacon, before anything else, is a doer—a minister and facilitator of the charity of a parish or of a diocese. At the core of his identity as a servant is the beautiful call to the first deacons, recounted in the Acts of the Apostles. Fittingly, this passage is included in the readings for the Fifth Sunday of Easter, Year A:

> As the number of disciples continued to grow, the Hellenists complained against the Hebrews because their widows were being neglected in the daily distribution. So the Twelve called together the community of the disciples and said, "It is not right for us to neglect the word of God to serve at table. Brothers, select from among you seven reputable men, filled with the Spirit and wisdom, whom we shall appoint to this task, whereas we shall devote ourselves to prayer and to the ministry of the word." The proposal was acceptable to the whole community, so they chose Stephen, a man filled with faith and the holy Spirit, also Philip, Prochorus, Nicanor, Timon, Parmenas, and Nicholas of Antioch, a convert to Judaism. They presented these men to the

apostles who prayed and laid hands on them. The word of God continued to spread, and the number of the disciples in Jerusalem increased greatly; even a large group of priests were becoming obedient to the faith. (Acts 6:1-7)

This passage has some complicated spots, and it is often quoted without them. However, if we are to really understand the ministry of the deacon and to understand charity as the primary part of the ministry of the deacon, we should look at this passage in its entirety, exactly as it appears on the Fifth Sunday of Easter.

To begin with, some Scripture scholars say that this passage is not really clear in establishing the diaconate as an office in the Church. Certainly, seven persons are chosen "to serve at table," that is, to oversee "the daily distribution." But the seven who are chosen are not called deacons. The title, for which we presume an office, only appears later, in Romans 16:1, in Philippians 1:1, and in 1 Timothy 3:8-13.

The passage from Acts reflects a problem that arose in the early days of the Church. One group of early Christians—those who spoke Greek, or "the Hellenists"—believed that the widows of another group of early Christians—those of the Palestinian Jewish Christian community, or "the Hebrews"—were getting better treatment. The Christian community as a whole was determined to assist widows in charity. But factions arose, and soon so did a dispute. The apostles, "the Twelve," called the community together and created the first corporate entity specifically devoted to the ministry of charity. The apostles, to be sure, knew they had to oversee the charity of the Christian community, but they could not manage the specific tasks involved and still attend to the necessities of public prayer and of preaching the Gospel. So they asked the community to choose who would manage the food, money, and goods devoted by the whole community to the needy, in this case to the widows of both the Hellenists and of the Hebrews.

There is a very important point here that is often overlooked: it is the community who calls forth these seven people. Stephen, whom we all recall as both the first servant and the first martyr, is joined by Philip, Prochorus, Nicanor, Timon, Parmenas, and Nicholas of

Antioch. The community presents these seven trustworthy souls, known undoubtedly for their honesty and energy, to the apostles. It is then, and only then, that the apostles lay hands on them. Are these seven the first deacons? Or are they the first lay executives of Catholic Charities?

To tell the truth, they are probably a little bit of both. The nascent Church did not have clear structures, as we do today. It is clear that the deacons of history are not identical to those who live the diaconate today. No matter. These seven and all who followed are they who, in the ancestral lineage of our tradition, were specifically called forth to be devoted to charity. The diaconal works of the ancient Church were many: "Now Stephen, filled with grace and power, was working great wonders and signs among the people" (Acts 6:8) but was killed.

Thus Philip went down to [the] city of Samaria and proclaimed the Messiah to them. With one accord, the crowds paid attention to what was said by Philip when they heard it and saw the signs he was doing. For unclean spirits, crying out in a loud voice, came out of many possessed people, and many paralayzed and crippled people were cured. (Acts 8:5-7).

Stephen, Philip, and the others, along with the women deacons (Paul specifically called Phoebe a deacon, not a deaconess, of the church at Cenechrae) provided as well for the needs of the people and assisted the apostles in their mission and ministry.

Questions for Reflection

1. How are the first deacons examples for deacons today?
2. Does your local Church understand and support the diaconate?
3. How can you make the diaconate better understood?

Endnotes

✠ ✠ ✠

1. John Mary Vianney, "Catéchisme sur la prière." A. Monnin, *Esprit du Curé d'Ars* (Paris, 1899) 87-89.
2. *Rites of Ordination of a Bishop, of Priests, and of Deacons* (Second Typical Edition). (Washington, D.C.: USCCB, 2003) 143.
3. Congregation for the Clergy, *Directory for the Ministry and Life of Permanent Deacons (Directorium pro ministerio et vita diaconorum permanentium)* (Washington, D.C.: USCC, 1998) no. 23.
4. The International Theological Commission's new document on the diaconate notes that deacons were chosen by the bishop to do whatever he found necessary— "beaucoup de choses nécessaires." "Le Diaconat; Évolution et perspectives," *La documentation catholique* (19 Janvier 2003: 58-107, 69).
5. Congregation for Catholic Education, *Basic Norms for the Formation of Permanent Deacons.* (Vatican City: Libreria Editrice Vaticana, 1998) §9.
6. Pope John Paul II, Post-Synodal Apostolic Exhortation, "I Will Give You Shepherds" *(Pastores dabo vobis).* (Washington, D.C.: USCC, 1992), no. 30.
7. Congregation for the Clergy, *Directory for the Ministry and Life of Permanent Deacons (Directorium pro ministerio et via diaconorum permanentium)* (Washington, D.C.: USCC, 1998), no. 28.

Further Reading

✠ ✠ ✠

James M. Barnett, *The Diaconate: A Full and Equal Order*. New York: Seabury, 1981.

Congregation for the Clergy, *Directory for the Ministry and Life of Permanent Deacons* (*Directorium Pro Ministerio et Via Diaconorum Permanentium*) (Washington, D.C.: United States Catholic Conference, 1998).

Richard R. Gaillardetz, *A Vision of Pastoral Ministry* (Liguori, Mo.: Liguori Publications, 2002).

Pope John Paul II, *The Heart of the Diaconate: Servants of the Mysteries of Christ and Servants of Your Brothers and Sisters*, address to deacons of the United States, Detroit, Mich., September 19, 1987.

Pope John Paul II, *The Permanent Deacon's Ordination*, address to the plenary assembly of the Congregation for the Clergy, November 30, 1995.

Phyllis Zagano, "Examen of Consciousness: Finding God in All Things." *Catholic Update,* St. Anthony Messenger Press, March 2003.

Phyllis Zagano, *Holy Saturday: An Argument for the Restoration of the Female Diaconate in the Catholic Church* (New York: Crossroad/Herder, 2000).

"Le diaconate, évolution et perspectives", Commission Théologique Internationale. *La documentation catholique*, 19 janvier 2003: 58-107.